THE TRUE VALUE OF A

Woman

Twelve Guiding Principles

The True Value of a Woman Twelve Guiding Principles
by Bishop Larry Jackson
Copyright © 2014

Breastplate Prayer Publications
Distributed by Frontliners Ministries
3715 Ridge Road
Charlotte, NC 28262

Cover Design: Family First Designs; www.FamilyFirstDesigns.com
Editing/Format: AbleAnnie Administrative; www.ableannie.com

Printed in the United States of America
ISBN: 978-0-9857687-9-9

Twelve Guiding Principles

Principle One: *A Valued Woman has come to understand that she was created to worship God first and her entire heart is centered on Him.*

✦

> *And the LORD God said, It is not good that the man should be alone; I will make him a help meet for Him.* **Genesis 2:18a**

The woman's creation was in direct relationship to Genesis 2:15 where we find Adam dressing and keeping the Garden. The word dress in the verse is the Hebrew word "Abad" which means Levitical type of worship. God decides that man should stand not in worship alone and makes the woman primarily to join him in worship and to protect the place of their worship.

In Luke chapter 4 verses 21 thru 24 Jesus discusses and gives the only definition of worship to the Samaritan at the well.

> *Jesus saith unto her, Woman, believe me, the hour cometh, when ye shall neither in this mountain, nor yet at Jerusalem, worship the Father. [22]Ye worship ye know not what: we know what we worship: for salvation is of the Jews. [23]But the hour*

cometh, and now is, when the true worshippers shall worship the Father in spirit and in truth: for the Father seeketh such to worship him. [24]God is a Spirit: and they that worship him must worship him in spirit and in truth. **John 4:21-24**

Jesus gives us the keys to worship, in His encounter with the woman at the well, which no one else had heard from Him. That worship has two ingredients; Spirit and Truth. I find it very interesting that He shares this with a woman that is living in an ill advised relationship and who has been married seven times. This is the kind of woman most religious people would turn away from but Jesus tells her how to have a deeper and more intimate relationship with God through worship.

It is clear this is what was taking place in the garden as the Man and Woman functioned as one with their full attention on God and His greatness while at the same time loving each other.

This first principle is the foundation of the True Value of a Woman movement because it is one of the main reasons the woman was created and it is the place she must find again because her voice is needed to give adoration and glory to God alone.

Jesus is asked about the greatest commandment and He discusses how our entire being must be completely centered on God which is the very essence of worship.

> *And he answering said, Thou shalt love the Lord thy God with all thy heart, and with all thy soul, and with all thy strength, and with all thy mind; and thy* neighbour as thyself. **Luke 10:27**

Every part of our being is designed to worship the Lord God and it is the place of worship that the enemy doesn't want man to find because it instantly diminishes hell's influence and ability.

Remember, if Satan wants it then that thing must be very important to God, man's success or both.

> *And the devil, taking him (Jesus) up into an high mountain shewed unto him all the kingdoms of the world in a moment of time. And the devil said unto him, All this power will I give thee, and the glory of them: for that is delivered unto me; and to whomsoever I will I give it.* **If thou therefore wilt worship me**, *all shall be thine.* **Luke 4:5-7**

When a husband and wife join together in worship it completely causes confusion in hell. It brings more of the divine presence and authority into their lives and dwelling place. It is time to worship together, Father is seeking for you!

Personal Testimony from Minister Vanessa Briggs, National Director Principle One

My life is complete because of my worship relationship with the Lord. I make it a point on a daily basis to spend time with the Lord by reading my bible, reading Christian literature, and by taking time to sit and worship Him. It is my daily connection with Him.

I love God and I talk to Him about his greatness, telling Him how much I appreciate Him. I do this when I get up in the morning, as I walk the halls at school or simply when I'm taking walks on a Saturday morning. Because I do this consistently God keeps me strong so I don't waver or fall because of the attacks of the enemy.

I have found that as a woman of God, and a worship leader pursuing the heart of God that I am a threat to the enemy. It has been because of my intimate relationship with the Lord that I have been able to overcome the enemy.

When my marriage was under severe attack and the enemy tried to literally take my husband's mind and kill him, it was because I worshipped the Lord in the midst of it all that not only saved my marriage, but my husband's life as well. I felt like I was coming apart too, but because I never stopped meeting with the Lord and worshipping Him, He kept me and restored me and my husband.

I can't imagine not spending time with the Lord. I am a woman who knows how to worship the Lord when times are good and when times are not good. I am passionate about worshipping God. It is all I live for and it is a priority for me. I protect the place of my worship, and when I do I am protected and all those who are connected to me are protected.

How I've Applied This Principle in My Life

> It is in the process of being worshipped that God communicates His presence to men.
>
> *C.S. Lewis*

_____

_____

_____

_____

_____

_____

Principle Two: *A Valued Woman is committed to reaching beyond any racial and denominational barriers to demonstrate the power of biblical unity*

+

> *Neither pray I for these alone, but for them also which shall believe on me through their word; 21That they all may be one; as thou, Father, art in me, and I in thee, that they also may be one in us: that the world may believe that thou hast sent me. 22And the glory which thou gavest me I have given them; that they may be one, even as we are one: 23I in them, and thou in me, that they may be made perfect in one; and that the world may know that thou hast sent me, and hast loved them, as thou hast loved me.* ***John 17:20-23***

With so many different denominations and sects associated with the body of Christ it would seem it is impossible for true unity to be developed. It is clear that Jesus wouldn't have prayed this prayer if it was impossible and we know that all things are possible with God.

This prayer is recorded so that everyone in the body of Christ would know what was prayed and even though it was a prayer spoken over the disciples which extends to us today, I believe women can sometimes find this place sooner than men as they as far more willing to commune together without competition. This unity must be developed beyond the local church walls with a Kingdom of God mindset. This doesn't mean the local church isn't important and should be cast aside but sometimes it is the walls that hinder unity instead of promoting unity.

Women will fellowship and love one another even when they come from different churches and races many times without the bias seen and found among the brethren.

> *For ye are all the children of God by faith in Christ Jesus. [27]For as many of you as have been baptized into Christ have put on Christ. [28]There is neither Jew nor Greek, there is neither bond nor free, there is neither male nor female: for ye are all one in Christ Jesus.* **Galatians 3:26-28**

Paul gives us the key to biblical unity and it has three ingredients; release to God your culture, your rights, and your gender. Then we will be found "In Christ" as one new man so making peace.

In the past I've used a glass filled with water and a bucket filled with water to demonstrate this point. You have heard and may have used the term "filled with the Spirit of Jesus". I liken the glass filled with water to these terms and then use a spoon to stir the water very fast, while the water is moving I will place the glass holding the water down to demonstrate that the glass doesn't move even with the water's movement.

This is much like many who indicate they are filled with the Spirit, even when He is moving or trying to move them they don't respond.

Then I take the same glass and submerge it into the bucket filled with enough water to fully cover the glass. This time the glass is filled to the over flowing and is also completely surrounded by water. This time when the water is stirred the glass moves with the stirring of the water. The water that is filling the glass is also controlling the glass it is filling.

Now if you put a different shaped glass or different color glass in the bucket all of the glasses will be filled by the same substance and controlled by the same substance and therefore connected in unity by the same substance.

It is time for us to live in the "Bucket" of Jesus and allow Him to be the unifying substance of our lives.

Personal Testimony from Donna Ebron
National Director Principle Two

"In most situations, my first instinct is to check to see if there are military persons within eyeshot, because I was brought up as a third generation military child. My grandfather was in the Army, my father was in the Marine Corps, and my husband had 25 years in the Marine Corps. I have spent most of my life in a "military bubble." Although racial barriers existed in my life I didn't actually feel them until I set foot off base.

In my lifetime the opportunity to engage with friends who were multicultural, enriched my life. We were friends based on character as opposed to ethnicity. I was exposed to all types of people and cultures. Therefore we all had a sense of oneness and the ability to be of one mind, one spirit and one body. Let me explain further. Our houses were all the same, just a different color. Our dads and some moms all wore the same uniform. Our parents were of the same economic background. In essence, that oneness is what enabled the ability for us to "be" of one mind, one spirit, and one body.

Currently I work as a residence coordinator for a lively community of senior citizens, aged 62 and older. I assist them in their desire to be independent for as long as possible. The community I serve is extremely diverse. One day a gentleman named Hung Lu came to my office in a large degree of pain. As he sat down to share his heart with me he conveyed his concerns about his health. He was most definitely in a place of hopelessness.

He'd begun to describe his humble needs, and of the $125.00 a month given to him by his relatives. He also had no health insurance, and he lived in constant pain every day. He shared with me that he'd had cancer 7 years ago, and that it was back. He hung his head and began to weep. As I watched a 75 year old Chinese man weep in front of me, I knew only God could fix this situation.

I asked him what he knew about Christianity. He said that he was in the United States for six years and he was a Buddhist, but he attended a Christian church once. This gave me the opportunity to explain to him who God was to me. I told Hung Lu that his situation can only be fixed by God. I then proceeded to ask him if we could pray. He said, "Yes" and "to please ask your God to help me."

We held hands and asked the Lord Jesus Christ to help, to give guidance, the right doctor, a program, and that along with whatever Hung Lu needed would be less than $50.00; we also asked God to stop his pain in order for him to live a painless life. After I prayed I asked Hung Lu "Do you believe what I just prayed?" He replied, "I will watch and see what Donna's God does."

Three weeks later a lady who works in the next office stopped by to talk to me and I told her about Hung Lu's situation and how we prayed and asked God to open up the doors for us. She then called her husband, who was a physician's assistant that helps people with no insurance and low wealth. I signed Hung Lu up and 2 weeks later we had an appointment to see a doctor. He had two doctor visits and a scheduled surgery all within two months after the prayer. Hung Lu was grateful and kept thanking me, but I kept referring him back to my God. Since then he refers to Jesus Christ, as "Donna's God." He said "Donna's God is Good! Donna's God is awesome"!

He was able to receive all treatments and a clean bill of health for a total of 47 dollars..."MY GOD is good!" This act of God's love has spread throughout the Chinese community whereby they ask me about Jesus Christ all the time. I was an open vessel that God used in a very sensitive situation. I thank God for being able to share his love with Hung Lu and in his situation. I pray for more Chinese people now than I have in my lifetime.

Please read these scriptures before answering the following questions.

John 15:9-20
John 13:34-35
Leviticus 19:11-18

> *12 My command is this: Love each other as I have loved you. 13 Greater love has no one than this: to lay down one's life for one's friends. 14 You are my friends if you do what I command.* **John 15:12-14**

As you look at yourself and your daily journey through life does your love show the world GOD'S true love; Is GOD conditional or unconditional in his assistant and love to all races and denominations?

How I've Applied This Principle in My Life

> *The Cross is the ultimate evidence that there is no length the love of God will refuse to go in effecting* **reconciliation**.
>
> R. Kent Hughes

_____

_____

_____

_____

_____

Principle Three: *A Valued Woman is positioned as a help meet with her husband to announce their purpose to the entire generation*

✛

> *I will make him an help meet for him.*
> **Genesis 2:18b**

The Word for Help Meet in this verse is the Hebrew words "Ezer and Neged" which mean helper and one in front of, straight forward, before, in sight of.

This is a difficult principle to get across to most people because of the fall of mankind and the shift that happened with the man and woman. Before the fall man and woman are given dominion and the ability to subdue over the works of God's hand but not over each other.

After the fall man is given dominion over the woman but not the ability to subdue. This change changed the equality of the man and woman and it is instantly reflected throughout the scripture. For this reason there aren't any natural examples of the woman functioning as a helpmeet to her husband.

Thank God for Jesus who destroyed the works of hell and restored all that was lost even the relationship between the man and woman. He didn't just redeem and restore the fallen man but man and woman.

Jesus functioning as the last Adam also needed a wife to make the restoration complete. He birthed the church out of His death, burial and resurrection as His bride. The church now functions in the place with Christ that Mrs. Adam functioned before the fall and each of us who live in Christ as married people now demonstrate this relationship to the world.

Submitting yourselves one to another in the fear of God. [22]Wives, submit yourselves unto your own husbands, as unto the Lord. [23]For the husband is the head of the wife, even as Christ is the head of the church: and he is the saviour of the body. [24]Therefore as the church is subject unto Christ, so let the wives be to their own husbands in every thing. [25]Husbands, love your wives, even as Christ also loved the church, and gave himself for it; [26]That he might sanctify and cleanse it with the washing of water by the word, [27]That he might present it to *himself a glorious church, not having spot, or wrinkle, or any such thing; but that it should be holy and without blemish. ²⁸So ought men to love their wives as their own bodies. He that loveth his wife loveth himself. ²⁹For no man ever yet hated his own flesh; but nourisheth and cherisheth it, even as the Lord the church: ³⁰For we are members of his body, of his flesh, and of his bones. ³¹For this cause shall a man leave his father and mother, and shall be joined unto his wife, and they two shall be one flesh. ³²This is a great mystery: but I speak concerning Christ and the church. ³³Nevertheless let every one of you in particular so love his wife even as himself; and the wife see that she reverence her husband.* **Ephesians 5:21-33**

- How do you speak about your husband and the purpose of God for him?

- God has given women the ability to affect a man's heart in way that nothing else can. Women who learn the art of "the sound" find that things that once seemed difficult in their relationship are now easy.

- I understand that he may not be showing you the love you want and maybe he can't even get there but are you doing your part? (*This statement takes for granted that there is no abuse taking place*)

  Likewise, ye wives, be in subjection to your own husbands; that, if any obey not the word, they also may without the word be won by the conversation of the wives; ²While they behold your chaste conversation coupled with fear. **1 Peter 3:1-2**

In the original design of marriage the woman would be positioned as a help meet in full oneness with her husband and they would worship God together and accomplish the vision of God as one!

What many women don't realize is that men need them to be unified with them; it causes men to accomplish the difficult things in life. His first concern is if his wife is with him then his full attention can be placed on defeating or solving the task at hand.

A new spirit of oneness is needed within our marriages to be modeled to our nation.

Personal Testimony from Sandy Ralya, National Director Principle Three

When I met Tom, he swept me off my feet, and I eagerly agreed to be his wife. Throughout our short engagement, I observed things in him that concerned me, but I overlooked them—I was getting married! We could work on the rough edges later. On a cold December day, Tom and I passionately vowed our lives to one another forever.

It wasn't winter's icy winds that cooled my passion to love, honor, and cherish. It was my inability to deal with Tom's rough edges grating on my own. Marriage is all about becoming one, and I had no idea how to make that happen. I needed help.

I had heard good teaching at church, but I didn't understand how to make the information practical and relevant to my situation. I was afraid to talk about my marriage and expose its rotten spots; everyone else's marriage seemed so good. Ill-equipped and isolated, I responded to my marriage problems with what came naturally to me: preaching at Tom. When preaching didn't work, I got angry or withdrew my love to signal my hurt or disappointment. That didn't work either, and it made us both miserable.

After eleven years of suffering, I decided there had to be a better way of dealing with the problems I faced rather than simply protecting myself from getting hurt or retaliating in anger. I turned toward God and began studying His Word. I also revealed my secret pain to others. God used His Word and wise women—friends, family members, and a Christian counselor—to mentor me, which enlarged my understanding of my role as a wife. As I learned and grew, I made choices to reverse negative cycles that had plagued me for years. When I gave God the control over my marriage relationship, He accomplished in five months what I couldn't in eleven years. He turned our marriage around and began the process of healing it.

Who can you turn to when you're struggling with marriage issues? Where do you find the practical advice you need to make a good marriage great? What is God's truth concerning your role as a wife?

My experience parallels a biblical plan for strengthening marriages. In Paul's letter to Titus, he stresses the importance of three things for married women: turn to God, understand your role, and share within a community of women.

> *As for you, promote the kind of living that reflects right teaching. . . . Teach the older women to live in a way that is appropriate for someone serving the Lord. They must not go around speaking evil of others and must not be heavy drinkers. Instead, they should teach others what is good. These older women must train the younger women to love their husbands and their children, to live wisely and be pure, to take care of their homes, to do good, and to be submissive to their husbands. Then they will not bring shame on the word of God. (Titus 2:1, 3—5 NLT)*

If you follow this threefold plan, healing will break forth in your life, just as it did in mine. It doesn't matter whether your marriage is an oasis, a desert, or something in between. God faithfully uses a community of women and these principles to heal, strengthen, and encourage you.

My book, *The Beautiful Wife,* offers biblical principles, practical tips, and inspiring stories to guide and encourage you as you look for God's best in your marriage. Chapter 5 is my signature chapter which asks women to TRACE a new path for their feet if they don't like the results they're experiencing in their marriage. I base the need to trace a new path on Hebrew 12:13

Trust instead of Control

Respect instead of Demean

Appreciate instead of Criticize

Confer confidence instead of Doubt

Expose vulnerability instead of Defensiveness

Visit www.beautifulwomanhood.com to find all the tools you need to strengthen your marriage as you build loving, godly, and supportive relationships with other wives.

How I've Applied This Principle in My Life

***Marriage** is a total commitment and a total sharing of the total person with another person until death.*

Wayne Mack

_____

_____

_____

_____

_____

_____

Principle Four: *A Valued Woman is full of integrity and lives her life in the standard of holiness*

+

Follow peace with all men, and holiness, without which no man shall see the Lord: **Hebrews 12:14**

The aged women likewise, that they be in behavior as becometh holiness, not false accusers, not given to much wine, teachers of good things; **1 Timothy 2:3**

This is a subject that can be completely overlooked in today's church involvement. Every subject is talked about in abundance except for holiness. Since God is holy then HE requires each person connected to Him to holy.

Speak unto all the congregation of the children of Israel, and say unto them, Ye shall be holy: for I the LORD your God am holy. **Leviticus 19:2**

Women must help to keep the standard of the holiness of God in the hours since the enemy is using women to entice by using the spirit of seduction through every medium he can.

Holiness is not a doctrine it is a lifestyle and it is sad to say that many in the body has approach a holy life style as out dated or belonging to a denomination. Holiness is beautiful and isn't even connected to long dresses and black suits, it is not an outward garment but an inward quality.

> *Whose adorning let it not be that outward adorning of plaiting the hair, and of wearing of gold, or of putting on of apparel; 4But let it be the hidden man of the heart, in that which is not corruptible, even the ornament of a meek and quiet spirit, which is in the sight of God of great price. 5For after this manner in the old time the <u>holy women</u> also, who trusted in God, adorned themselves, being in subjection unto their own husbands:*
> **1Peter 3:3-5**

Integrity

A firm adherence to a code of ethics, Values, an unimpaired condition, soundness, undivided, completeness, honesty

Holiness

The state of being hallowed or consecrated to God, sacredness (Israel was holiness unto the Lord)

As a child I received Jesus Christ as my savior and was taught scriptures every week in Sunday school. I remember the story of Daniel, a man of integrity, exiled from Israel, taken to a Babylonian country serving a heathen king. But regardless of his situation he still prayed three times a day to Almighty God. Because of Daniel's integrity and consecration to God, he would not yield to the laws of the land to worship the king. As a result, he was thrown into the lion's den, then protected through the night by an angel.

To a kid of ten, someone being rescued by an angel...how cool was that?!! I admired him for his integrity and I seriously wanted to try to mirror the prayer life of Daniel, who was holy and set apart for God. I could plainly see he was a blessed man, so after the Sunday school lesson, I went home and began to pray. My desire was strong and my resolve was set, I was going to pray on my knees three times a day and it was lookin' good!

It only took two days for all the hot air in my prayer balloon to dissipate and for my commitment and resolve to wither, thus, no Daniel! I should let you know, there was a good reason to stop, because as a child, the only prayer I knew was "Now I lay me down to sleep, I pray the Lord my soul to keep".... and you know the rest. Three times a day "Now I lay me down to sleep" became old real quick and BORING! As a 10 year old, my desire was good, but the reality was I had not developed a relationship with God to fuel my prayers or my spiritual motivation.

Daniel's integrity, holiness and resolve were developed as result of his relationship with his God. His unwillingness to bow was because of his knowledge and love for the law of his God. That is what made Daniel stand out above all the governmental leaders of his day. It was holiness and integrity and they are still relevant for us today. Holiness is not religious do's and don'ts. It is the condition of the heart that takes place when we become born from above. Through Christ Jesus we are a Holy Priesthood to minister unto the Lord our God. We grow in holiness as we allow the Spirit of Holiness, the Holy Spirit Himself, to inhabit our heart and desires. And we are holy because He sets us apart for his service; not as the result of religious traditions.

Integrity is not given by the laying on of hands, nor is it a spiritual gift. It is a very valuable virtue developed in the life of a believer. Integrity is not part of a packaged gift we receive with salvation, but is built within us through testing, trials and pressures. This process is overseen by the Lord himself. Much like the making of a very high quality automobile, let's say a Ferrari.

First comes the frame work, then step by step things are added. Every piece is pressed or tempered and molded, then carefully put together in proper order. At the end of the process there is an incredible, well-built vehicle of great worth. A Ferrari's integrity goes before it; this is always the goal of the manufacturer. The car is built with excellence so people will want to own one. The problem with a Ferrari is the price tag. Most everyone would love to own a Ferrari, but they are not willing to pay the price.

The development of integrity and holiness is pretty much the same, they can be quite costly, but they hold great value when developed in our lives. I have seen this take place in my life, in the darkest days of my life when I could turn to no one but Jesus, all because of a vow that I had taken. The Lord did not wave a magic wand and make it all better, nor did it go away, but He gave me a strength I didn't know that I had to endure isolation, hardship, slander and persecution.

Like Jesus we are not to try to escape from sufferings, even though I wanted to, I ask for His grace to endure through them; thus the pressing and molding. This process holds a very powerful place of authority in the Kingdom of Heaven, just look at the lives of the prophets and apostles. Integrity and holiness are evident in my life today as I stand in the roll as prayer pastor, leader and teacher to encourage, influence and lead others in the kingdom. These qualities are definitely not the status quo portrayed neither in the social media nor in our modern culture. But these are God's standards that need to be raised up in the Church of Jesus Christ. Integrity and holiness may sound old school, but they are not!

True Holiness and True Integrity will never be worn as badges of honor, paraded through the streets to gloat or celebrate. But, rather they are observed as mantles of strength, drawing others to Christ who is the source of these treasures.

How I've Applied This Principle in My Life

A baptism of **holiness**, a demonstration of godly living is the crying need of our day.

_____

_____

_____

_____

_____

Principle Five: *A Valued Woman will work to recover as many women as possible to their original design*

✦

> *Do not neglect to do good and to share what you have, for such sacrifices are pleasing to God.* **Hebrews 13:16**

> *Let each of you look not only to his own interests, but also to the interests of others.* **Philippians 2:4**

> *Give, and it will be given to you. Good measure, pressed down, shaken together, running over, will be put into your lap. For with the measure you use it will be measured back to you.* **Luke 6:38**

This principle is the active evangelistic focus of the movement! Since women naturally share with each other even when they don't really have a close relationship; in the store, at work and even at play, it is important that the True Value women stay focused on this task.

A true sisterhood must be developed that surpasses the gender issue to reach the hearts of other women. It is for this reason that women must be reached with the message of value so that their hearts are reconnected to the One who created them.

God wants His daughters repositioned in oneness with the man and He placed them in the upper room with the men, at the tomb with the men and even had them carrying a message to the men.

Awakening women to who they are as women is very important but once they are reconnected to their creator with full assurance that He will be there for them, this will be an unstoppable army that will help bring the church together in ways that we have been waiting for.

It was one woman who helped the disciples assemble together so that the Lord could visit them and give their marching orders.

Sharing this principle with young women who will be used to share what a True Value woman looks like will shift the generation and develop a new generation of women who will be able to stand against the wiles of hell.

It is time to recover women who are beaten down, confused, have lost hope, angered, embracing the dirt lifestyle and who can't believe they are valuable to God!

There are so many women who need to hear that they aren't created from dirt and who need to understand the womb issue. Things will also become clearer when they realize hell has a special hatred for women even above the hatred it has for men.

> *And I will put enmity between thee and the woman, and between thy seed and her seed; it shall bruise thy head, and thou shalt bruise his heel.* **Genesis 3:15**

This enmity can be seen everywhere women are concerned but it isn't talked about much not even in the church. It is time to spread the word and prepare your sisters to fight back with their full armor on.

Personal Testimony from Apostle Wendy Becton, National Director Principle Five

Women are the handiwork of God. This valuable, distinguished entity plays a vital part in what God has purposed for man. We are, by nature, designed to incubate and bring forth God's manifested purpose in the earth realm. Each woman must gain an understanding of who she is if she is to execute her kingdom assignment with excellence. She walks into her destiny with a realization that God has ordained her for greatness. A woman can only be fulfilled when she recovers her original status. She is destined to exert dominion over every aspect of life. When a woman knows who she is, she is able to influence other women. She endures and embraces the dealings of God, knowing what the process will yield. A valued woman emerges from each challenge with a God given authority. She speaks and operates in a kingdom authority that wreaks havoc on the forces of hell. She allows God to use her as a vessel of honor and strength in a weak and dying world. A woman who has become enlightened and empowered by Truth is able to influence other women. This is true ministry.

Jesus set the ultimate example of ministry by operating in the power of humility. He, being in the form of God, did not consider it robbery to be equal to God. He took on the form of a servant, and came in the likeness of men. He humbled himself and became obedient to the death of the cross (Philippians 2:6-8). Our Lord is able to feel our infirmities because He experienced every facet of the human experience; from pain to temptation. He learned obedience through the things He suffered. God has given me the same passion for ministry. I have received a kingdom mandate to effect change in the lives of hurting women. My witness is authentic and relevant because I have embraced the dealings of God. By His grace I have withstood, escaped and triumphed over the torment of abuse, the pain of rejection, and the oppressive darkness of witchcraft. These are but a few of the attacks that the enemy has launched against my destiny. Yet, God's plan prevailed! He weaved every trial into the tapestry of the purpose He set forth for me before I was placed into my mother's womb. He has given me beauty for ashes and the garment of praise for heaviness. I can now identify pain in those who are suffering, and I am anointed to bring the message of deliverance to women in bondage.

There was a call upon my life even as a small child. The enemy heard the prophetic proclamations uttered over me and set out to destroy me. I almost choked to death as an infant. I recovered from that attack only to face others. I was placed into a freezer and locked inside at age 3. I believe that fear entered into my spirit at that time, opening a door to overwhelming, pathologic anxiety. I became extremely fearful in ordinary situations. The fear kept me in bondage as a child, placing limitations on everything I tried to do. Each time I attempted to progress, fear would manifest. The voice of terror and defeat propelled me back into a state of apprehension and self-doubt. Finally a breaking point came. I was scheduled to have a MRI. I lay on the table as it slowly moved inside a huge, tunnel like machine. Panic instantly gripped me and refused to let go. I realized that day that a demonic stronghold had overtaken me. I asked the Lord to reveal to me the source of my distress. He took me back to my childhood and revealed to me the point at which the fear had entered in, leaving me vulnerable to the attacks of the enemy. The fear had reoccurring manifestations that intensified with each episode. I prayed for deliverance and God broke the power of that terrible phobia. I was released from bondage.

Consequently, I understand what it feels like to struggle under the weight of bondage. I am now able to identify that vicious cycle in others. I am called to look deep beyond the surface presentation that I see in the church to deal with the hidden depths of the soul. I have lead others to freedom because I have been liberated from those dark places myself. The hardships and afflictions I have suffered in life have processed me into my purpose. God did not waste any of that heartache and pain. It was used to train me to identify suffering in others. I can witness to the words of the Apostle Paul in 2 Corinthians 4:7 who declares that we have this treasure in earthen vessels, that the excellence of the power may be of God and not of us. I was hard pressed on every side, yet not crushed; I was perplexed, but not in despair; persecuted, but not forsaken; struck down, but not destroyed. The crushing only caused the oil of the anointing to flow so that excellent oil touches the hearts and souls of the hurting.

That oil affords me the ability to discern the ravages of pain. Sometimes I can see it. Sometimes it manifests as a certain sound and I can hear it. It pierces the harmony of the choir member's melodious song. It seeps through the smile that is plastered on the usher's face. It often transcends the surface presentation and manifests as a disturbance of the spirit. God used my pain to catapult me into my purpose. I will continue to work to recover as many women as possible to their original state. I can share the source of my victory with others. Worship has been my lifeline. It ushers me into a realm of peace where I am exempt from demonic assault and harassment. In His presence is fullness of joy.

God's desire is to birth many daughters into their kingdom destinies. This can be accomplished through preaching, teaching, counseling, and mentoring. The women as well as the men of God can and will conquer and reclaim territory for the Kingdom of God. Let us bring glory to God by maintaining a standard of holiness and encouraging others to recognize and follow the divine pattern of God.

How I've Applied This Principle in My Life

A woman is the full circle. Within her is the power to create, nurture and transform.

Diane Mariechild

_____

_____

_____

_____

_____

Principle Six: *A Valued Woman will not associate with dirt and will never allow herself to be treated like dirt*

✦

> *And the LORD God caused a deep sleep to fall upon Adam, and he slept: and he took one of his ribs, and closed up the flesh instead thereof; [22]And the rib, which the LORD God had taken from man, made he a woman, and brought her unto the man. Genesis [23]And Adam said, This is now bone of my bones, and flesh of my flesh: she shall be called Woman, because she was taken out of Man.* **Genesis 2:21-23.**

The number six is associated with man since it was on the sixth day man was created from the dust of the ground and God breathed into him the breath of life and he became a living soul.

Principle six of the True Value of a Woman movement is to remind women that they weren't created from the same material. God is not limited in any way and could have very well formed the woman from the dust of the ground in the same fashion He formed the man.

But He didn't and most people have never asked why.

I believe that He formed her from the side of the man for two reasons: 1. So that the man would value her as an equal. 2. So that she would know how much God valued her even though she wasn't created at the same time with the man.

Not being created from dirt means she shouldn't be treated like dirt by the man or anyone. She shouldn't associate herself with a dirty lifestyle that would devalue her before God and man. She shouldn't speak curse words and use disrespectful language to communicate her point. Her appearance must reflect the holy lifestyle of principle four and not bring attention to her body.

The dirty lifestyle is promoted all over the media and entertainment world as glamour instead of women embracing dirt. Since men love to play in the dirt this is very appealing to men and most will do absolutely nothing to change these women because of the desires of their flesh.

Again our young women and young girls must be taught this principle before they are completely indoctrinated by the prevailing culture. They must be taught that sex isn't primarily designed for men but for women and he doesn't have a right to experience anything sexual fulfillment with a woman until he gives his life for her in marriage.

You are not dirt, live as a valuable commodity!

Personal Testimony from Monique Johnson, National Director Principle Six

At the age of 21 as I approached my final semester in college I was in the midst of a rebellious stage against the Lord; and had embraced the dirt life. One night while at home in my apartment I received a call from someone that I knew through friends, but had no relationship with. He asked if he could stop by and hangout. In my heart I felt uneasy, but since one of my friends was already at my house, I allowed him to come over. After being there only thirty minutes my friend decided to leave and although I didn't want him to go, I was too afraid to ask him to not leave me.

Twenty minutes after the door closed the dirt that I had already subjected myself to from the rebellious life I had been living, became thick mud that could not be shaken, as the man began to rape me. At that moment, I felt he had taken the last part of me and there was NO WAY I could ever get it back. I did everything I could to try to remove the layers of dirt that came in my life in the form of shame, regret and worthlessness, all because I had laid down and had connected myself to dirt. I began drinking heavily in order to numb the physical, emotional, and physiological pain that I was feeling. I needed and desired something, anything that could help me forget the dirty person I had become.

Two weeks later I came home and told my mother what happened and she took me to the doctors, where the doctor performed a series of tests and examined me. He informed me that since I did not come in right away, the only thing they could see was that my uterus had been damaged. Already distraught, I would later receive a call from the doctor's office stating that I had contracted HPV. I knew there was only one way to experience healing and freedom from my past, so I rededicated my life back to the Lord. For years I went to the doctors to be tested and was told that this virus was incurable. The devil used this report to remind me of my dirty past, but I would not accept it. I believed strongly in my heart that the Lord had forgiven me and that He was going to heal me.

Years later, while attending a Watch Night service, my Pastor was talking to the congregation about how God wanted to burn up the things in our lives from the past. He told us to write down what we wanted God to burn up and place it on the altar. All of a sudden the memories of the dirty life I had led, came flooding back. My mind raced with thoughts of what people would say if they knew my secret. With GREAT fear gripping my heart, I took a step of faith and I wrote on a small piece of paper HPV and took it up to the altar. Immediately, the Pastor picked up some of the papers, (mine being one of them) and lit them on fire. He said that he was showing us a picture of what God was doing for us, which was burning up the things of the past. I claimed that word for my life and believed that I would be healed.

I left the service and while driving I began to have this burning sensation in my stomach, as if it were on fire. Within two weeks I went to the doctor and asked to be tested again. She said you will always have HPV, but she went along with my request and performed the test. She called me a few days later and with a surprised voice said "You no longer have HPV." *Isaiah 61:3 became my testimony for God had given me beauty for the ashes in my life.*

If you were anything like me, you allowed the enemy to trick you into thinking that the dirt level was a fun place to be. Often we try to rationalize our level of dirt by comparing it to another. However dirt is dirt whether it is the thoughts you entertain about what you want to do or you act on your feelings, giving parts of yourself away to anyone who will give you attention. The True Value of a Woman Guiding Principle 6 helped me to see that I not only associated with dirt, but I allowed myself to be treated like dirt, because I bought into the tricks the enemy had gotten me to believe about myself.

As I began to minister to young women I realized that this was not just an issue that I faced, but that many young women face all over the world. How could I combat the dirty female images that Hollywood and the music industry deemed as normal? How could I change the mindset of a generation of young women who desperately wanted to be loved and were willing to do anything to receive it? The only way was to share with others what the Lord had done for me. So I started a young women's ministry called Inner Court Ladies for girls ages 12-21. Each girl was different and had a unique past. I saw God transform their lives, as I shared my story and taught them that they were precious daughters of the Lord. As they went off to college some struggled with the constant pressure of dirty living all around them.

Many of you have a similar type of story and you desire God to clean you up, because you have found yourself living on a type of dirt level. God does not play favorites. If He healed and forgave me, He can and will do the same for you. There is nothing too GREAT and nothing too horrible that you or someone else could have done to you to change His mind in forgiving you and making you brand new. So my question for you today is; are you ready to step out of the dirt and into the cleansing arms of Jesus? He is the one person that will cleanse and forgive you from ALL of your dirt!

How I've Applied This Principle in My Life

*When a woman embraces a dirty
lifestyle she loses the value God
provided her*
                Bishop Larry A. Jackson

_____

_____

_____

_____

_____

Principle Seven: *A Valued Woman understands the need for community involvement*

✦

> *In all things I have shown you that by working hard in this way we must help the weak and remember the words of the Lord Jesus, how he himself said, 'It is more blessed to give than to receive.'* **Acts 20:35**

> *And whatever you do, in word or deed, do everything in the name of the Lord Jesus, giving thanks to God the Father through him.* **Colossians 3:17**

One of the ways people outside of the kingdom can see and understand our Lord Jesus is through seeing Him in the believer. This means that the church must function outside the walls of the local buildings they gather in. Taking an audit of the community where you live is very important so that the needs in that community can be met.

A plan that is designed to minister to the felt needs must be well thought out since many of the people in the community will not trust the efforts of the church in many cases.

But there are places that will embrace your desire to help such as; nursing homes, prison ministries, pregnancy centers, senior centers and schools. This is an opportunity to serve and not be served.

> *But someone will say, "You have faith and I have works." Show me your faith apart from your works, and I will show you my faith by my works.* **James 2:18**

> *Whoever brings blessing will be enriched, and one who waters will himself be watered.* **Proverbs 11:25**

As a movement we must be relevant in the communities around us. Keeping our ears and eyes open for the opportunities to join community efforts will help to break down walls.

Because most people are so protective over the things they are involved in, they are very guarded when outsiders come with sincere hearts to help.

But the more we help and can get endearments from other organizations the more these guarded organizations and ministries will open up.

Our Lord told us that it is more blessed to give than to receive, and that the greatest person is the one who serves. Communities are hurting for servants that they can depend on with a true desire to see change take place for those who live there.

That is who we are and what we do!

Personal Testimony from Prophetess Donna Stalling, National Director Principle Seven

Deborah, Esther, Abigail, Ruth, Rahab, Rispah, 'A certain woman', "the woman at the well," and the Proverbs 31 woman each have a common thread that exudes from their existence. It is called "legacy community with business acumen." Whether their stations are found in the king's palace or sitting under a tree their faith brought divine strategy and longevity to their communities and nations' existence – through a womb of love and influence. Their unyielding faith in an unlimited God, escorted through fears, societal pressures and legalistic restrictions. Each was pregnant with relentless concern that unleashed an extraordinary relationship with the Lord and uncommon favor. These women (along with many others) remain to be the examples of understanding the true purpose of a woman's God-infused influence and its VALUE -- which extends far beyond the borders of immediate family, but down through generations and thus to the community of God. A woman of value understands they are anointed as prophetic solutionists, and mid-wives as well as merchandise importers and exporters (that is for another time).

I have ministered in pulpits throughout the world, but my greatest love is to sit in a room with hopelessness or despair and just begin to unlock the gates of hell that will not prevail. As a child I was very gifted but was MIA (missing in action) and entered into a atmosphere where the assignment was to develop my calling into a drug addict or alcoholic, paranoid, abused girl who had been molested, beaten by strangers, and literally put in chains. Yet, in my darkest moments my value was always emerging even then as a torch of VALUE and PURPOSE while we were yet in sin. In search of me, I found that the community offered every offense, sin, death, drugs, parties and false alignments. It is by God's grace that the very drug and lifestyle that was intently placed in the community to destroy my generation – could not and did not prevail. I was born for greatness yet had the possibility of becoming a drug drowned leader. BUT GOD turned my captivity captive. The enemy's assignment was to cause me to miss-carrying the glory needed for my assignment. BUT GOD turned it around. This change is ignited through a relationship with my Father that even as I write brings me to a safe place and a place of power. I carry an assignment with a mantle to go back and teach and impart Jesus in communities where low self-worth, prostitution, parentless street and foster children, at-risk girls and boys, mothers who want to quit and unsaved souls are waiting for God.

My community passion came first through the example of my own mother, Gladys Stallings, who was an avid fighter for the less fortunate. She instilled the necessity to fight for the community. As children we marched in front of slumlords property where a family lived without toilets; we practically lived in our wonderful home church, which was also the community center where children and seniors were cared for. Even though I was a young girl participating in every social march, sitting in meetings where I witnessed self-less leaders strategize, I was a rebel – because I did not have the spirit of God alive in me as of yet. I was infused with disgust and unbridled emotions for those who treated others unjustly. Yet without this community center, I can't phantom where my life would have been. At sixteen, I went on a field trip to an Indian reservation where – instead of enjoying the games and activities -- my eyes only saw the injustice and my group leader forced me back on the bus, because I was marshalling the Indians to fight back for their land. A womb of compassion – but with crushed emotions. So, I went into a strange world of lost souls who did not know their value. And believe me, it is a miracle, that through the right hand of God, I was snatched out right on time. SOMEBODY PRAYED FOR ME.

In July 1989, something miraculous happened – the Holy Spirit filled my soul, and Jesus Christ truly became my Lord and Savior. I began to study the word of God in search of me; In search of answers to all of my whys; in search of His confirmation; and in search of that dunamis power that I had witnessed. I stayed in the prayer room for weeks and weeks (years) until I was broken out of shame and into the life for which I was born. There was a woman there, Mother Dalton, who imparted intercession and a prophetic release. This moment merged my mother's compassion with the Lord's direction and protection. I can remember very clearly the day that I heard the spirit of God say to me "feed my sheep." Acts 2 had come alive and the fire of God set right on top of my value. I was like the woman at the well. I went back to the places that were holding my friends and family captive, and they would immediately see the light of God. Love was activated that day, purpose came alive and through His grace, after twenty-five years, I continue to live a surrendered life as "a weapon in His hand" (Is. 49:2).

My ministry began first in prayer and then in the prisons and jails in our state. For seven years, the group of us went into the prisons and youth homes where we witnessed the power of God. Then on the street where I sat in a restaurant and saw three young, beautiful prostitutes come in to eat. The Lord opened my eyes and my heart to see VALUE – even though their outer appearance suggested otherwise. I cannot reveal the entire encounter, but their words will forever be in my heart as I left... I turned to the one who received Christ (that's right in those clothes) and said to her "I love you." Immediately, the other girls asked me "don't you love me too?" This is the cry of the community – WHERE IS THE LOVE? As God's women, we carry the communal love and can powerfully activate grace through it. His compassion empowers ministry of salvation right in the cleaners, in business encounters, while making a purchase at a corner store counter, – just last night we stood in front of a grocery store and led a young person to Christ. The community is ready and creation is groaning for us to appear.

My life's mission is to serve as a catalyst for kingdom dominion and a voice of hope as God sends me into the community and through my travels abroad to spread the message of love, reconciliation and living with purpose. I am not afraid to go into places where captives are being held hostage. With all of the professional awards and accolades, nothing compares to understanding that we are SOLUTIONISTS for our community and our nation. The pain is now power; the chains are broken and is now character; the fear is now faith; the low self-worth is now VALUE. What the enemy meant for evil, through the COMMUNITY and His CHURCH, I am free. As I embrace many platforms of men, women and children – whether in the church house, in the street or business encounters, the antidote is the same -- JESUS and Holy Spirit. Praise God for His faithfulness. A woman of value must infiltrate and affect their community for the kingdom!

How I've Applied This Principle in My Life

Law; an ordinance of reason for the common good, made by him who has care of the community.
Thomas Aquinas

_____

_____

_____

_____

_____

Principle Eight: *A Valued Woman is a woman who understands how to earn or advance monetary resources*

✦

She seeketh wool, and flax, and worketh willingly with her hands. [14]She is like the merchants' ships; she bringeth her food from afar. [15]She riseth also while it is yet night, and giveth meat to her household, and a portion to her maidens. [16]She considereth a field, and buyeth it: with the fruit of her hands she planteth a vineyard. [17]She girdeth her loins with strength, and strengtheneth her arms. [18]She perceiveth that her merchandise is good: her candle goeth not out by night. [19]She layeth her hands to the spindle, and her hands hold the distaff. [20]She stretcheth out her hand to the poor; yea, she reacheth forth her hands to the needy. [21]She is not afraid of the snow for her household: for all her household are clothed with scarlet. [22]She maketh herself coverings of tapestry; her clothing is silk and purple. **Proverbs 31:13-22**

This is an important principle and can be the very thing that helps to destroy the wiles of hell. Over the last 20 years there has been a move away from men in our society and many men have felt it and have allowed resentment towards the system to overtake their hearts.

One of the ways this has been done is by advancing women past men and many women have taken this opportunity to develop an attitude that they don't need the man. In this way hell wins and we can't let this attitude to continue. What is meant for evil will be turned to the good!

But when the marriage covenant is understood then this plan backfires on the enemy because the woman and man function as one. The man will do everything in his power to help his wife increase because it is "them" who are increasing.

The wife will never put down or make her husband feel less than a man because of money or earning potential.

There are more and more women owning their own businesses, becoming executives and overseeing major corporations who have a kingdom of God mindset; women in the marketplace who are there to reach others and to advance ministry. Jesus had women who followed Him much like His disciples but these women supported His ministry.

> *And it came to pass afterward, that he went throughout every city and village, preaching and shewing the glad tidings of the kingdom of God:and the twelve were with him, And certain women, which had been healed of evil spirits and infirmities, Mary called Magdalene, out of whom went seven devils, And Joanna the wife of Chuza Herod's steward, and Susanna, and many others, which ministered unto him of their substance.* **Luke 8:1-3**

The women in Luke 8 were women of means and they used these means to further the kingdom with their support of the Jesus' ministry. These were unmarried women but they had the same focus; kingdom advancement!

Women in business and women who work for someone else must have a kingdom advancement mindset in this hour. It is our goal to help women understand how to advance their businesses and how to start businesses but all of this must be done with the right attitude so that hell is proven wrong again.

We clearly know that the world will not function in this way that is the reason why they will take note and our light will shine so bright in the marketplace.

Reach out to women in your community who own their own business and invite them to a local meeting where the *True Value of a Woman* book is being discussed so that they can understand their value and start to live the principles. In each case where you find women who have ministries, businesses or just a desire to work within one of the 12 guiding principles, please get them connected with the National Director over that principle, especially those you find in the marketplace.

Many of these women have felt that they are alone in their efforts and need as much support as we can give them. Let's go to work!

Personal Testimony from Elisabeth Braswell, National Director Principle Eight

As I sit here and read principal eight the first thing that comes to my mind is that I was a woman who understood how to earn and advance monetary resources BUT I found my VALUE in that. I have been an entrepreneur for as long as I can remember. I love ideas, creating, building and seeing something grow. The problem was, even as a strong believer, I had it all backwards. My identity was wrapped up in what I DID, how well I performed and produced and I sought after recognition from man to determine my worth. In May of 2008, as we seemed to have the world by the tail...a beautiful home, thriving careers, a lake house, serving in ministries in various capacities...but that was all about to change.

A three day supernatural encounter with The Lord turned EVERYTHING upside down and inside out. What looked extraordinary and grand three days earlier now was lackluster and not enough. I knew our lives, as we knew them, were about to be radically changed. I could not have imagined to what extent or even begin to grasp what the next 6 years would hold. Overnight, my business brain and any desire to "be" who I was trying to "be" three days earlier literally disappeared. Subsequently, I disappeared. We were told by the Lord to put our house on the market. The realtor told us houses in our price range were not selling. The Lord told us to list it at $888,000 and TWO WEEKS LATER on 8/8/8 our house was under contract and we were underway to a wild ride of following the Holy Spirit like our lives depended on it...and they did!

For two years, it was just me and Jesus. The prophetic opened up in a profound way. Dreams, visions, revelation, healing...anything and everything that had given me identity, value, or worth was stripped away and it got very, very real. I had to re-learn and re-cover the truths about who I am and my identity as a daughter, a VALUED WOMAN OF GOD. This is the first step that is CRITICAL if we, as women of God, are going to venture into the marketplace to make an impact. The world system and all of its trappings are thick with promise and pull. Knowing WHO YOU ARE, WHAT you are CALLED to (not just what you can do), and WHO IS IN YOU is the only way to survive in the mine field of the marketplace.

Six years. Removed. Tucked away. Learning. Hearing. Discovering. During this season, The Lord began to talk to me about FIELDS. He showed me that the marketplace was a field I was going to be called to go back into. He had rescued me to go back in and rescue others. One morning He showed me a scripture:

"Then Boaz said to Ruth, You will listen, my daughter, will you not? Do not go to glean in another field, nor go from here, but stay close by my young women. Let your eyes be on the field which they reap, and go after them." Ruth 2:8

Two days later my phone rang. A lady I had done training for years earlier called me out of the blue. She was about to buy a 23 year old company that had 15,000 women IN THE FIELD and she wanted me to come and pour into, train and equip. Wow. Overnight, after 6 years, I was launched back into the field as if no time had passed at all.

The lesson in all of this is that we can trust God. When He says stop, stop. Trust the time. Wait. When He says go, go. But constantly, as we go, we must know that we go IN HIM. Tucked in and on a mission to advance the kingdom and to do things in the complete opposite spirit of the world system. We are going to see a great move of God OUTSIDE THE WALLS of the church buildings. A harvest happens in the FIELDS not in the buildings. We are to be in those fields, to stand out and look different, act different and carry change. When we go into the marketplace in a posture of knowing who we are, who is in us and WHY we are there everything shifts and opens up a path before us. It's a beautiful thing to affect the atmosphere and places we go instead of being affected by them. THIS is how we will learn to not only advance monetary resources, but advance the kingdom.

How I've Applied This Principle in My Life

If women didn't exist, all the money in the world would have no meaning.

Aristotle Onassis

Principle Nine: *A Valued Woman loves men for their God given abilities and strengths*

✦

Let no man despise thy youth; but be thou an example of the believers, in word, in conversation, in charity, in spirit, in faith, in purity. **1 Timothy 4:12**

But thou, O man of God, flee these things; and follow after righteousness, godliness, faith, love, patience, meekness. **1 Timothy 6:11**

There is a tendency when women fellowship together with the focus of advancing women causes that the subject of men somehow comes up. It has long been a plan of hell to separate men and women from functioning as one and this was clearly accomplished through the fall.

Once this plan was accomplished the man and woman became combatants and not allies, something that we can still see today especially when a couple has to walk through circumstances. We encourage women to deal with the hurts and issues that they have dealt with where men are concerned and understand that flesh and blood isn't the enemy and come to the understanding that the true enemy dwells in hell.

God gave the vision of this movement to a man and there is no way that the True Value of a Woman movement can have a negative attitude toward men. There is no male bashing in this movement and never will be! She loves men for the way God has designed them and she allows them to be that man.

We do understand that many men still need to be trained in the area of manhood and that it is also the plan of hell that has moved from this understanding through a host of different traps' and circumstances. Without any doubt men have been a source of many problems where women are concerned. But forgiveness is the key to women helping men come to the place they are designed by God to be.

Guiding Principle 3 speaks to the married woman but also applies to all women in the way they learn the "Sound" to move the heats of men.

Likewise, ye wives, be in subjection to your own husbands; that, if any obey not the word, they also may without the word

be won by the conversation of the wives;
1Peter 3:1

It must be taught that the way to a man's heart is through his ears and not through his stomach. And he will do whatever is needed to hear a woman speaking to him that way again.

The True Value woman understands how to speak peaceably to the men in her life and her environment. She will help them to stay focused on God and will encourage them in this area because she understands the man's place as a spiritual leader.

> *In all things shewing thyself a pattern of good works: in doctrine [shewing] uncorruptness, gravity, sincerity, Titus 2:7*
>
> *"Be watchful, stand firm in the faith, act like men, be strong. Let all that you do be done in love." 1 Corinthians 16:13-14*
>
> *"Therefore, my beloved brothers, be steadfast, immovable, always abounding in the work of the Lord, knowing that in the Lord your labor is not in vain." 1 Corinthians 15:58*

Personal Testimony from Bishop Larry Jackson
National Director Principle Nine.

One of the television shows that I enjoyed watching during my childhood was "The Beverly Hillbillies." Because I watched the program daily, it wasn't long before the words of the theme song became a part of my memory.

I will come back to the show in just a minute. Over the last 17 years I have been vitally involved in the Men's Movement that has help to sharpen and increase scores of men across North America.

My own men's ministry "Frontliners Men's Ministry" was birthed in 1999 and is still functioning today in several church communities across America. Men frequently approach me as I travel to report how our Lord helped change their lives through a particular message that I've spoken.

Father God has given me a unique way to minister to men and it's a wonderful thing to watch a man turn from sin to follow Jesus Christ our Lord!

The other place I've focused during this time is to help city leaders understand how to work together for the Kingdom advancement. Because many of these leaders are men my main focus has been kept on men and the issues facing their lives.

During my years working with Promise Keepers Men's Ministry, one of my primary messages was to men concerning marriage. The goal of the messages were to teach men how to lead their wives into the face of Almighty God and how to serve them as Christ serves and loves the church

In my role as a local Pastor, I understand how important it is to have strong marriages and families for the overall stability of the church. Because marriage is under great attack today from the prevailing culture, information that helps couples understand their roles and responsibilities to each other is greatly needed.

For this reason, we developed a marriage class that meets twice a month before the Sunday morning service and it is a great success. It is one of the best attended classes at the church and it always has a great deal of excitement surrounding it.

The revelation that God gave me concerning women began to free the hearts and minds of the women attending the classes. They indicated that all of the women in our church should know what they were learning and asked if I would have a special meeting to share that information.

Our church has a dynamic women's ministry, "Women of Zion," overseen by my wife. The Women of Zion ministry is connected to our Fellowship of International Churches organizational women's ministry, "Kingmakers," under the leadership of Bishop Wellington Boone, who has written a book by the same title.

For these reasons, I didn't want to have another meeting that would compete with these two vehicles that were doing just fine in my estimation. But the women in the class wouldn't let it go so I finally gave in and told them if they pulled it together I would do it.

With virtually no advertisement, only word of mouth and a short last minute You Tube video, our church was full of women from all across the city.

During the time I was preparing for the one day meeting, something came alive in my heart and I realized that God was the one setting all of this up, not the women, which takes me back to The Beverly Hillbillies television program.

In the theme song, Jed Clampett sings that he "...was shooting at some food and up from the ground came a bubblin' crude. Oil that is, black gold, Texas tea." He was trying to meet one small need and an entirely different and much larger need was supplied!

That is how I feel about the information in this book. It wasn't what I was looking for, but it is what God gave to meet the need of so many women and even men. The reports we have received from those attending the meeting as well as those who have listened to the recorded messages have been tremendous.

Men have listened and indicated that they had no idea that God has valued women in the way He has. I have shared the message in men's meetings and they have actually run to my product table to purchase the recordings that were taught to the women.

It is my prayer that the information in this book will help you in the same way. So now it is your time to tap your well of oil that is waiting deep down inside of you. If you are a woman reading this book, please understand that God has never made any invaluable person or thing, so start thinking of yourself like He sees you!

God Bless!

How I've Applied This Principle in My Life

God is not looking for extraordinary characters as His instruments, but He is looking for humble instruments through whom He can be honored throughout the ages.

A.B. Simpson

Principle Ten: A Valued Woman helps to mold and guide her children into greatness

✦

> Train up a child in the way he should go; even when he is old he will not depart from it. **Proverbs 22:6**

> The rod and reproof give wisdom, but a child left to himself brings shame to his mother. **Proverbs 29:15**

> Behold, children are a heritage from the Lord, the fruit of the womb a reward. Like arrows in the hand of a warrior are the children of one's youth. Blessed is the man who fills his quiver with them! He shall not be put to shame when he speaks with his enemies in the gate. **Psalm 127:3-5**

The nurture of a mother is something that can never be overrated. Children are the heritage of the Lord and they must be discipled into godly men and women. The society has so attacked the family financially that it is difficult for the wife and mother to remain home to help raise her children.

Because both parents have to work much of the training is left up to non-family members. These may be good people with a great business model but it is still not mommy and daddy. When both parents must work it is important to spend time with the children to teach them the biblical principles that will help govern their lives.

During their formative years this is very important but once a children enters school with all of the peer pressure that will come it is of great importance that parents spend time talking with their children about how they are processing life. It is the Adamic nature for man to lie and hide things but parents must make it known to the children that they have the freedom to share what is happening with them and their friends. Once they do so you must show them that you respect them for sharing and not overreact to what you learn.

This will help when and if you have to deal with a situation that they share. Always remember to show your children the biblical reference so that they will know it is not just an opinion of yours but a principle from God!

A mother and daughter relationship can be confrontational at times. Many would say it is due to two women occupying the same space, but I would remind you of the hatred fact and how much hell hates women. Keeping this relationship strained doesn't allow the older women to train the young in ways to recognize and defeat the enemy.

Notice how often the teenage children in the movie or television show are disrespectful or play a character that is downright selfish and even dumb. A great deal of the time it is the female children that play this role. Why is this? Hell hates women!

Mothers, it is time to train your daughters and sons concerning this fact. They can't fight you because they haven't heard about it from anyone so it is new information to them and this generation loves new information.

Play a neat game with your children to point out when the movies, television and entertainment worlds try to paint teens in a negative light.

Stay active women of God in prayer for our children and the generational gap will get much smaller!

Personal Testimony from Julie Hiramine, National Director Principle Ten

So people always ask me how did Generations of Virtue begin here I was a mom I had three children then they were 8, 5, and 2 and I was pregnant with number 4. As I looked at my kids and I realized in the past that I had done youth ministry and led a lot of youth with the YMCA I realized that so many of the kids that I worked with, what their parents did while they were in preschool and elementary school and early middle school made a huge impact on the choices they made throughout middle school high school and college. So as I was thinking about that and asking God what do I do? Here I have these kids that are growing up in a completely different world than I ever grew up in it's a completely different world than even when I was a youth pastor.

So what do I do now? How do I handle the issues and the challenges that they have? And as I began to seek the Lord I began to pull together some books and I began to think okay how do I want to put them in their character how do I want to talk to them about things about sex and do that age appropriately while their younger. I

94

listened to everything I could find and I sought out resources and as I did them and put together what I was going to do with my children, God said to me Julie this is not just for you. There are so many parents who face this who are struggling. They don't know what to they don't know how to raise kids in this culture.

Believe me I'm the number one chicken when it comes to talking to my kids about sex, I shake I do things like I take deep breaths and I look at the words and say how could I ever say this to them but God just began to say look this is my whole plan this is my idea, sex is my idea them being raised and walking against the tide of culture is how I want to see your kids.

And that is how generations of virtue got its start is on my knees. It is a place where God just began to download and say look these are the things that kids need to know. This is what will be helpful.

It's interesting to look back. You know now I have an 18 year old, and a 15 year old, and I have 5 children going down to the age of 5. But now I have a direction and I speak to thousands of parents not only here in the United States but all over the world. Parents love their kids our heart is for our children. We want to see them succeed;

we want to see them making healthy choices. We want to see them walking with God and fulfilling their call and their destiny.

And so what we need to do is begin saying how do I do that? How do I do that from day one? And so that's been my passion with Generations of Virtue. It's not only about being pure out here, it's not about being pure in body or looking pure or acting right or saying the right things. This is about a message that goes much deeper than outward actions. This is a message that starts in the heart and renews the mind with the word of God. And then goes out in action. This is a message that is about purity of heart, purity of mind and purity of body. It's not just about putting on a good show.

And so this is a group that can come to you and show you in practical ways how to help your kids walk in that way. How not just to act the right way but for Christ's love to be deeply anchored inside them and for a future love story in their life to have the foundation of Jesus Christ and not just a foundation that the world acts out that says that you should do it this way or that way but what does the bible say about having a true love story and a true romance. And I say that love story starts with the Lord Jesus Christ. And that is where we need to start with our kids.

www.generationsofvirtue.org

How I've Applied This Principle in My Life

The secret of homemade rule is self rule, first being ourselves what we want our children to be.
Andrew Murray

_____

_____

_____

_____

_____

_____

Principle Eleven: *A Valued Woman is concerned and involved in women's suffrage around the world*

+

> *Rejoice with them that do rejoice, and weep with them that weep.* **Romans 12:15**

> [37]*Jesus said unto him, Thou shalt love the Lord thy God with all thy heart, and with all thy soul, and with all thy mind...* [39]*And the second is like unto it, Thou shalt love thy neighbor as thyself.* **Matthew 22:37 & 39**

In our world there are many ways women are experiencing suffrage. Bride kidnapping is a common practice in Kyrgyzstan and Turkmenistan. Honor Killing is a punitive murder, committed by members of a family against a female member of their family whom the family and/or wider community believes to have brought dishonor upon the family. A woman is usually targeted for: refusing an arranged marriage, being the victim of a sexual assault, seeking a divorce (even from an abusive husband), or committing adultery or fornication.

Bride Burning is a form of domestic violence practiced in parts of India, Pakistan, Bangladesh and other countries located on or around the Indian subcontinent. In bride burning cases it is alleged that a man, or his family, douses his wife with kerosene, gasoline, or other flammable liquid, and sets the woman alight, leading to death by fire.

Acid Attacks are violent phenomena that primarily occur in Afghanistan.

Female genital mutilation refers to all procedures involving partial or total removal of the external female genitalia or other injury to the female genital organs whether for cultural, religious or other non-therapeutic reasons.

Since the fall of the iron curtain, the impoverished former Eastern bloc countries such as Albania, Moldova, Romania, Bulgaria, Russia, Belarus and Ukraine have been identified as major trafficking source countries for women and children. Young women and girls are often lured to wealthier countries by the promise of money and work and then reduced to sexual slavery.

In parts of Ghana, a family may be punished for an offense by having to turn over a virgin female to serve as a sex slave within the offended family. In this system of slavery of ritual servitude, young virgin girls are given as slaves in traditional shrines and are used sexually by the priests in addition to providing free labor[1].

Human Trafficking isn't something you hear about on the evening news or the 24 hour news channels but it is very real and exploding in growth. Most people don't even know this is taking place in their own cities and towns.

The number of trafficking victims in the US is largely unknown. However, hundreds of thousands of US citizen minors are estimated to be at risk of commercial sexual exploitation.

A great number of missing cases has to do with human trafficking where the women or girl is taken into a foreign place or land where they are beaten and made to perform sexual acts against their will.

This movement is focused on praying for these women and helping them by joining with the many programs, agencies and ministries

---

[1]*http://listverse.com/2008/06/10/7-terrible-abuses-suffered-by-women-around-the-world/*

working on behalf of our sisters across the world.

One of the greater problems can be where a woman is trapped even in a Christian relationship and is experiencing physical, verbal and mental abuse. Everything can appear to be going well on the outside but it is hostile at home.

We must find and help these women to find a place of freedom. It will be our goal to support centers and shelters to provide much needed getaways for these women and their children.

Then there are those who have emotional trauma extending from many situations that could be helped with the right people working with them and a people praying for them.

This principle is one designed to bring healing but is positioned right in the middle of the spiritual war zone. Thanks be to God that we have our armor and our Lord has won the war.

Personal Testimony from Stephanie Briscoe, National Director Principle Eleven:

I was 30 years old and had just moved to Washington, DC, as a newly married and then mother of two when I received a phone call from a cousin I hadn't spoken to in over 15 years. I was shocked that he even had my number. So when I asked him where he got it from he said my mother gave it to him. Annoyed with my mother for giving him the number yet curious as to why he needed to speak with me I continued the call and my life was never the same once I got off the phone. I remember it as if it were yesterday when he said, "I just wanted to hear your voice. Man its crazy down here in North Carolina. The cops came and tried to press charges on me saying I molested my daughter. I know my wife is trying to get revenge because of the divorce and what's worse my daughter is coming forth saying it was done to her."

Never did I think I would feel such a pain in my chest as I did in that moment, because as he was talking my entire childhood was replayed before my eyes. In total shock I said to him, "You did it to me! You made me lose my virginity at 8 years old because you had me believing this is what everyone does and no one will know." He replied, "C'mon that doesn't count we were kids and we didn't know any better." He was right I didn't know any better but he did and what didn't help is my mother walked in on us. She made him get up and sent us to our rooms. Today she says she thought she was doing the right thing by sending him away and he was never welcomed in our home again.

Startled at the fact that nothing was said or dealt with I longed to find out what was so wrong. Still on the phone I began to cry as if I was that little girl again fearful, needy and emotionally abandoned. My husband grabbed me and asked, "What is the problem." He took the phone and yelled, "Whoever this is she can't talk right now!" and hung up. We talked and I reminded him of what we discussed before, I was always told that I was "boy crazy" (someone actually bought me a tee-shirt with this saying on it) and "always seeking attention" (old folks called it being a fast-tail little girl). I even remember a cousin fondling me at a young age but was unsure of the details at the time.

It was during that call where I realized how it all happened. I went from feeling empowered to ashamed, ridden with guilt and sadness. It made sense now why my entire life I had struggled to be me. Hearing my family members making comments like "You got to watch her" was embarrassing but again no one came to my defense. The endless cheating and pointless relationships in my life; dating drug dealers, the opportunity to become a stripper to pay for my college (in that world this occupation was top grade), all made sense to me now. I was lost before I even knew I existed.

After reflecting through all that, the most important question I had was why didn't my mother ever talk to me about that night? Why didn't she console me, chastise me, or even educate me? It allowed me to see why our relationship from that point forward never was the same. Walking around in silence not knowing or understanding the depths of what happened shut me down intimately. Never being able to experience virginity or even fight for it crushed my spirit. Hanging with crowds that I knew weren't for me. Hiding behind a mask in church as the music director and faking it with my family left me with a void. Then in this madness I wondered, where was my father? Working and providing not knowing how to emotionally connect is the best answer to that. With all this hurt, all this baggage I was broken. I thought I had arrived; I rededicated my life to Christ, I have a husband who loves me, children and in-laws who understand me; my story was finally making sense at least that is what I thought.

It was in that moment during that call my journey to healing started. I had to bridge the gap to where I was then into who I am today. It wasn't my doing but the Lord's doing. In order for me to do His will I needed to have full understanding of my entire life (up until this point that is) so that I can travel the depths of another's soul and help bring them to a place of reckoning. He created me to be a guide and a messenger for the hurt and lost souls of today. My journey, my discovery, my passion to be a part of a movement that brings women from a place of bondage into a place of healing and forgiveness is what I am branded to do.

Helping women to know their rights and empower their voice is only the beginning. Women's suffrage has always been coined for the women's right to vote but its early start was as a group of clubwomen who sought self-improvement on the social, economic and political front (nwhm.org, 2007). This self-improvement later turned to reform efforts. Those efforts today touch so many different portals for the cries of a broken woman. My story is someone else's story and my exposure is a way to someone else's healing.

References:

"Reforming the World: Women in the Progressive Era." The National Women's History Museum. N.p., n.d. Web. 6 June 2014

http://www.nwhm.org/online-exhibits/progressiveera/suffrage.html

How I've Applied This Principle in My Life

Trouble's makes us kin.
                                    George Eliot

_____

_____

_____

_____

_____

_____

Principle Twelve: _A Valued Woman is committed to prayer, study and obedience to the word of God_

✦

Our Father in heaven, Hallowed be Your name. Your kingdom come. Your will be done On earth as it is in heaven. Give us this day our daily bread. And forgive us our debts, As we forgive our debtors. And do not lead us into temptation, But deliver us from the evil one. For Yours is the kingdom and the power and the glory forever. Amen.' **_Matthew 6:9-13_**

'Do not be anxious about anything, but in everything, by prayer and petition, with thanksgiving, present your request to God. And the peace of God, which transcends all understanding, will guard your hearts and your minds in Christ Jesus.' **_Philippians 4:6-7_**

Study to shew thyself approved unto God, a workman that needeth not to be ashamed, rightly dividing the word of truth. **_2 Timothy 2:15_**

It is the glory of God to conceal a thing: but the honour of kings is to search out a matter. **Proverbs 25:2**

There are many times in the bible where things are listed that the final word, principle, or statement is the one holding all of the weight. This could be where we get the term "saving the best for last" from.

Notice that Jesus mostly dealt with covetousness in teaching against desire and want. Covetousness is the tenth of the Ten Commandments. But is easy to connect that fact that if covetousness is avoided then none of the other Commandments would be possible.

It is much the same with these 12 guiding principle where number 12 is the foundation of all of the principles.

Prayer can't be something done only while at church but must be a staple in the life of the True Value woman. To free women from bondage we must first free them in the prayer closet. I've been known for prayer most of my ministry life and it was very fitting that a book on prayer would be my first publication. My book, *Numbered with the Transgressors,* is designed to free those people who the enemy really believes he has secured in his grip.

The Power is in the Closet is my book on the type of prayer that God says He would reward openly; praying in secret. Many intercessors have come out of the closet in an attempt to be better positioned in the church but God wants them to stay covered so that hell or the world can't find them and in that they can remain more affective.

With an increased dedication to prayer it must be based on God's word. We want to pray back to God His word and not our opinions and complaints. The bible tells us to study to show our approved unto God.

Women of the word and women of prayer are very powerful kingdom people.

Personal Testimony from Apostle Diane Chappelle, National Director Principle Twelve

Those committed to prayer, study and obedience to the Word of God would, more than likely, confess that those three components working together could probably be the one thing that has, or is becoming a strengthening and encouraging tool in these seasons of compounded challenges. I don't believe too many people are escaping the negative impact that life is throwing our way. Difficult days are not selective. We all have them. It would appear that some are hit harder and more consistently than others. But the reality is...life can hit hard!

Since becoming involved in the True Value Movement, I've had the opportunity to see the twelve guiding principles give direction, and encouragement to the women that have become involved, as well as other women being influenced by those involved.

As a leader in the Body of Christ, the twelfth principle has kept me aligned and positioned for the assignment before me. For all of us, if we are to be successful on these paths of life, whatever the assignment, there are tools that Father has given to assist us on the journey. Our first point,

Prayer, offers the one-on-one fellowship and communion that increases intimacy with the Father.

This building process, by way of personal encounter, has the ability to lift one into realms of wisdom, knowledge, and understanding that God desires to release to His vessels. Secondly, God's Word highlights His movement upon the Earth, and gives directives as to how one can make their life prosperous. We understand "prosperous" as defining lives that are complete, sound, well and peaceful. This is a constant state that is rewarded upon those who believe and follow His Word. It is through His Word that standards are set in which strengthens one in life encounters, and empowers them to topple the negative components of societal living. Prayer and the Word of God will bring one to our third emphasis, which is the proving ground of Obedience. For only as we are able to overcome in the face of temptations and other "obstructions", are we able to be victorious in the sight of God.

The True Value of a Woman's twelfth principle has not only strengthened me, but it has allowed me to be an encourager to others in ways that are termed, life-changing, supportive and sustainable. Whether in the Church, or outside of the Institution, we are empowered to help, even the unbeliever, to benefit from our personal encounters with the Father. Combining our Prayers with God's Word and our stamina in Obedience are given that we may be instruments in His Hand to release from bondage, those held in its grip. It is through the application of combined prayer, study of the Word of God, and walking in obedience, that one is given, and able to share the keys to life's successes.

How I've Applied This Principle in My Life

*Prayer is the link that connects us
with God.*

A.B. Simpson